LANCE ARMSTRONG

A Real-Life Reader Biography

Kimberly Garcia

Mitchell Lane Publishers, Inc.
P.O. Box 619
Bear, Delaware 19701

Mitchell Lane
PUBLISHERS

Printing   2   3   4   5   6   7   8   9

Real-Life Reader Biographies

Paula Abdul	Christina Aguilera	Marc Anthony	**Lance Armstrong**
Drew Barrymore	Tony Blair	Brandy	Garth Brooks
Kobe Bryant	Sandra Bullock	Mariah Carey	Aaron Carter
Cesar Chavez	Roberto Clemente	Christopher Paul Curtis	Roald Dahl
Oscar De La Hoya	Trent Dimas	Celine Dion	Sheila E.
Gloria Estefan	Mary Joe Fernandez	Michael J. Fox	Andres Galarraga
Sarah Michelle Gellar	Jeff Gordon	Virginia Hamilton	Mia Hamm
Melissa Joan Hart	Salma Hayek	Jennifer Love Hewitt	Faith Hill
Hollywood Hogan	Katie Holmes	Enrique Iglesias	Allen Iverson
Janet Jackson	Derek Jeter	Steve Jobs	Alicia Keys
Michelle Kwan	Bruce Lee	Jennifer Lopez	Cheech Marin
Ricky Martin	Mark McGwire	Alyssa Milano	Mandy Moore
Chuck Norris	Tommy Nuñez	Rosie O'Donnell	Mary-Kate and Ashley Olsen
Rafael Palmeiro	Gary Paulsen	Colin Powell	Freddie Prinze, Jr.
Condoleezza Rice	Julia Roberts	Robert Rodriguez	J.K. Rowling
Keri Russell	Winona Ryder	Cristina Saralegui	Charles Schulz
Arnold Schwarzenegger	Selena	Maurice Sendak	Dr. Seuss
Shakira	Alicia Silverstone	Jessica Simpson	Sinbad
Jimmy Smits	Sammy Sosa	Britney Spears	Julia Stiles
Ben Stiller	Sheryl Swoopes	Shania Twain	Liv Tyler
Robin Williams	Vanessa Williams	Venus Williams	Tiger Woods

Library of Congress Cataloging-in-Publication Data
Garcia, Kimberly, 1966-
    Lance Armstrong/Kimberly Garcia.
      p. cm. — (A Real-life reader biography)
    Includes index.
    Summary: A biography of the cyclist whose racing career was interrupted by a battle with cancer before he was back on track with a Tour de France win.
    ISBN 1-58415-125-0 (lib bdg.)
    1. Armstrong, Lance—Juvenile literature. 2. Cyclists—United States—Biography—Juvenile literature. Cancer—Patients—United States—Biography—Juvenile literature. [Armstrong, Lance. 2. Bicyclists. 3. Cancer—Patients.] I. Title. II. Series.
GV1051.A76 G37 2002
796.6'2'092—dc21
[B]
               2002022222

ABOUT THE AUTHOR: Kimberly Garcia is a bilingual journalist who found her first job at a newspaper on the U.S.- Mexico border because she spoke Spanish. Her paternal great grandparents migrated from Spain in the early 1900s to New York where her great grandfather edited an Anarchist newspaper. Garcia has a bachelor's degree in English and Spanish literature from the University of Wisconsin in Madison. After graduation, she worked for six years as a daily newspaper journalist covering crime, local governments and Hispanic-related issues in Texas and Wisconsin. Garcia writes for *Hispanic*, *Vista*, and *Latina* magazines, among other publications. She currently lives in Austin, Texas with her husband and two children.

PHOTO CREDITS: Cover: Corbis; p. 4 Joel Saget, Reuters; p. 9 AP Photo/Harry Cabluck; p. 14 Al Bello/Allsport; p. 19 Mike Powell/Allsport; p. 23 Chris Covatta/Allsport; p. 27 Doug Pensinger/Allsport; p. 28 Tom Able-Green/Allsport; p. 29 Stefano Rellandini/Reuters; p. 30 AFP Photo/Mike Theiler.

ACKNOWLEDGMENTS: The following story has been thoroughly researched, and to the best of our knowledge, represents a true story. While every possible effort has been made to ensure accuracy, the publisher will not assume liability for damages caused by inaccuracies in the data, and makes no warranty on the accuracy of the information contained herein. This story has not been authorized nor endorsed by Lance Armstrong.

Table of Contents

Lance Armstrong (shown here on the left) won four Tour de France cycling events (1999, 2000, 2001, and 2002) since being diagnosed with cancer. This photo was taken on July 18, 2000 in the French Alps with Frenchman Richard Virenque.

Chapter 1
The Race of His Life

Lance Armstrong was used to ignoring pain. As a world-class cyclist, he rode five or six hours a day, sometimes for weeks at a time, in all kinds of weather. He dared cold rain, blustery winds, snow, and even hail. Sometimes he rode for such a long time that every part of his body ached, from his neck, back, and hands down to his bottom, legs, and feet. Enduring pain is part of what athletes do to achieve greatness. So when his right testicle began hurting in 1996, Lance did what he was used to doing: He ignored it.

Eventually the symptoms surrounding Lance's right testicle became too difficult to bear. Lance coughed up blood in September, just a few days after celebrating his 25th birth-

Enduring pain is what athletes do to achieve greatness.

day. His testicle swelled to the size of an orange and became so sensitive that he could not ride his bicycle sitting down. He mentioned both problems to his physician, Rick Parker, a good friend and neighbor. Parker recommended that Lance see a specialist immediately. Little did Lance know when he went to see a urologist that he would find out he had cancer, both in his testicle and in his lungs.

Lance was in shock. He struggled to understand how cancer would affect his life. He wondered if he would live and if he would ever race again.

Cancer is a harmful growth that can spread throughout the body and kill its host if not detected and treated. Doctors treat cancer patients by removing the growth or by giving them chemotherapy. Chemotherapy involves injecting patients with toxic chemicals that kill cancer; the treatment can make the patient horribly ill. In Lance's case, doctors removed his testicle the day after his October 2 diagnosis and started him on chemotherapy for lung cancer a few days later. As if that weren't difficult enough, the worst news was yet to come.

Lance found out a week after surgery that the cancer had spread to his brain. Adding to his troubles, the hospital informed him he had no medical insurance. Lance was changing racing teams from Motorola to Cofidis. His new employer would not cover medical costs for cancer because it was a preexisting condition. Within two weeks, Lance went from being a wealthy world-class athlete to a troubled cancer patient wondering what he could sell to foot his medical bills.

Fortunately, Lance had a team of loyal friends and fans who lined up behind him in his fight against cancer.

Mike Parnell, CEO of Oakley, one of Lance's sponsors, went to bat for Lance over his health insurance. Parnell demanded that his health care provider cover Lance's medical costs, despite his preexisting condition, or Parnell would take his business elsewhere. The provider balked at first, but later agreed to Parnell's demand.

Dr. Steven Wolff, a cycling fan and head of the bone-marrow transplant department at Vanderbilt University's medical center, guided Lance with medical decisions. Wolff wrote to Lance with advice about tailoring his

Lance found out a week after surgery that the cancer had spread to his brain.

treatment to minimize possible side effects on biking. He also steered him toward the foremost doctors on the disease at Indiana University. Lance took Wolff's advice and traveled to Bloomington, Indiana, for treatment from oncologist Craig Nichols and neurosurgeon Scott Shapiro.

Lance was in good hands at Indiana University, medically and emotionally. Shapiro skillfully removed 12 tumors from Lance's brain. Nichols tailored Lance's treatment to preserve his balance and lungs for biking. Oncology nurse LaTrice Haney helped Lance hang on to his spirit. Her good humor, words of encouragement, and tolerance of his testiness won Lance's admiration. The two became so close that doctors let Haney give Lance the good news when his blood work came back normal after three months of chemotherapy.

But it wasn't just Lance's strong team of supporters who pulled him through the most important race of his life. Lance himself was strong and determined. He fought against cancer in the same way he races bicycles. The experience would make him a better human being and, one day, a better cyclist.

Lance was strong and determined. He fought against cancer the same way he races bicycles.

Here is Lance just one year after being diagnosed with cancer. He was getting ready to ride in a benefit for the Lance Armstrong Foundation, a non-profit organization to aid cancer research.

Chapter 2
A Disadvantaged Start

Lance was born to a single mom in Dallas, Texas in 1971.

Lance Armstrong has thrived despite adversity since the moment he was born on September 18, 1971, to a single mom in Dallas, Texas. His mother's maiden name was Linda Mooneyham. She was a proud, pretty, and determined 17-year-old who dropped out of high school to care for her son. People told Linda that Lance would never amount to anything, but Linda knew differently. She believed in turning every obstacle into an opportunity, and she taught her son by example to do the same.

Linda had nowhere to turn for help after Lance's birth. Her parents were divorced and her mother, Elizabeth, struggled to support three children. Her father, Paul, was a Vietnam veteran who worked at the post office and lived in a mobile home. He drank heavily until the day Lance was born. Paul gave up drinking then and has been sober ever since; however, he also did not help Linda with the baby. Linda's younger brother, Al, pitched in by baby-sitting Lance every now and then. Otherwise, Linda and Lance were on their own.

When Lance was a baby, he and his mother lived in a dreary one-bedroom apartment in Oak Cliff, a suburb of Dallas. Linda worked a variety of jobs, such as post office clerk and grocery store cashier, while finishing high school. The $400 she earned each month barely covered her $200 monthly rent and Lance's $25-a-week day care bill. Linda devoted to her son whatever time and money she had left over. She would hold him and read to him every night, even though she was tired and he was too young to understand the words. Linda's doting paid off. Lance walked by the time he was nine months old. He was reciting verses by age two and reading by age four.

Lance has never met his biological father. His mother married the man during her preg-

When he was a baby, he and his mother lived in a dreary one-bedroom apartment.

nancy, but the two split up before Lance was two years old. Lance and Linda did not discuss his biological father for the first 28 years of Lance's life. People were curious about his biological father once Lance became famous. Lance learned of his identity when a Texas newspaper reporter found out who he was and wrote a story about him. The article named him as Gunderson, a route manager for *The Dallas Morning News* who lived in Cedar Creek Lake and had two other children. Gunderson said he considered Lance his son, and his children considered Lance their brother, but Lance does not feel the same way. Gunderson's remarks struck Lance as opportunistic, and Lance wants nothing to do with him. Lance feels Gunderson gave up his legal rights to his son when he signed adoption papers.

Lance's adopted father is Terry Armstrong. Linda married Terry when Lance was three years old; Terry legally adopted Lance at that time. Lance was not crazy about Terry because Terry did not practice what he preached. Terry was a Christian who tried to convert others to Christianity. Meanwhile, he whipped Lance for small things, like being messy, and he cheated on Linda.

Linda did not tell Lance much about his biological father.

Lance found out when he was 14 years old about a relationship Terry was having with another woman. Lance and Terry were sitting in an airport waiting to take a plane to San Antonio, Texas, for Lance's swim meet. Terry was writing notes, crumpling them up, and throwing them away. Lance thought Terry's behavior was odd, so when Terry went to the bathroom, Lance retrieved the papers from the garbage can. Lance discovered that Terry was writing to another woman. Lance was particularly angry because his mother was in the hospital having a hysterectomy. He thought Terry should have been at the hospital with Linda, rather than writing letters to another woman at the airport.

Lance did not tell his mother about the incident then. Still, Linda and Terry decided to divorce a few months later, much to Lance's relief. Lance and Linda fared just fine on their own once again. Linda had been moving up in the workforce from secretary to account manager to real estate agent. The family also moved to Richardson, a northern suburb of Dallas, and then to Plano, an upscale suburb in which Linda had grown up. Terry continued to keep in touch with Lance, but Lance

Lance has an adopted father named Terry Armstrong.

eventually wrote him a letter to end the relationship. Lance managed to use his resentment toward Terry and others to his advantage, just as his mother had taught him. He tapped his angst for fuel in the athletic events that eventually consumed his life and afforded him a ticket to a luxurious lifestyle.

Lance has won numerous high-profile cycling events. He is shown here on May 3, 1996 during the Tour DuPont.

Chapter 3
Tapping His Angst

Lance has boldly poured all his energy into athletic events since the day he began competing. He became interested in running at age nine and joined the local swim team at age twelve. He needed so much work on his stroke at first that his coach made him swim with seven-year-olds. Still, Lance was not deterred. He leaped headfirst into the water at his first practice, and flailed up and down the pool as if he were trying to splash all the water out of it. His mother still gets choked up when she recalls how hard Lance tried that day.

Lance's hard work paid off. Within a year, he placed fourth in the state in the 1,500-meter freestyle, and he started entering long-dis-

> **Lance has poured all his energy into athletic events since the day he began competing.**

tance running competitions. He also rode his bicycle 20 miles each day to swim team practices. By the time he was 13 years old, Lance combined all three of his favorite sports to compete in triathlons. Even though he was young for a triathlete, he was one of the best in Texas by the time he was 15 years old. Triathlons boosted Lance's self-confidence and padded his wallet. Lance earned nearly $20,000 a year from winning triathlons. Still, the money was not enough. Difficulty finding sponsors to help pay for competitions and expensive equipment eventually dampened Lance's enthusiasm for the sport.

About the same time, Chris Carmichael of the U.S. Cycling Federation asked Lance, then 17, to join the junior national cycling team. Carmichael wanted Lance to train in Colorado Springs, Colorado, for the 1989 Junior World Championships in Moscow, Russia. Lance was thrilled about the idea of riding in his first international bike race, but administrators at his high school objected to his missing six weeks of school to train for it. Lance went anyway, and when he returned in March, school administrators made it difficult for him to graduate in June. Once again, he and his

Lance rode his bicycle 20 miles each day to swim practice.

mother refused to be deterred. Linda transferred Lance to a private school and he graduated on time, with the rest of his classmates.

Qualifying for Moscow did have a silver lining. His performance there led to invitations in 1991 to ride with the U.S. national cycling team and the Subaru-Montgomery Team. Lance, then 19, rode with the national team when he was abroad and with the Subaru-Montgomery Team when in the United States. Both teams developed amateurs into professional cyclists. Lance was just the cyclist to realize their mission. Within two years, he turned in a number of impressive performances and rose to the rank of world-class cyclist. His hallmark was a fiery but immature riding style. Sometimes he would sprint too soon and burn out before finishing a race.

As an amateur, Lance got a lucky break when he caught the attention of cycling pioneer Jim "Och" Ochowicz. Och noticed Lance during the 1992 Olympics in Barcelona, Spain, even though Lance finished 14th. He admired Lance's fire and offered him a contract to ride with a professional team sponsored by Motorola. Lance's admiration of Och soon

Lance got a lucky break when Jim Ochowicz noticed Lance at the 1992 Olympics in Barcelona, Spain.

The Tour de France is one of the most famous and grueling bicycle races in the world.

followed. He appreciated his vast cycling knowledge. Today he refers to Och as his surrogate father.

Cycling as a professional has had its ups and downs, notwithstanding the opportunity to earn millions of dollars. Cold rain during an arduous ride in Spain almost pushed Lance to drop out of his first race as a professional. He did drop out of the first Tour de France he rode in 1993, and in the 1995 Tour de France he lost a teammate, Fabio Casartelli, who died in a crash on the course. On the bright side, Lance won a stage in both races. The Tour de France is one of the most famous and grueling bicycle races in the world. Cyclists ride nearly five hours a day for three weeks and cover nearly 2,500 miles. Winning a stage means turning in the fastest time on one of those days.

Other highlights were earning a $1 million bonus in 1993 for winning three U.S. races in the Thrift Drug Classic. The same year, Lance also became at age 21 one of the youngest riders to win the World Championships in Oslo, Norway. As usual, his mother was a faithful spectator during both competitions. She sat for seven hours in the rain during the

World Championships. Lance remained loyal to his mother as well. He declined an offer to meet King Harold of Norway after winning the World Championships when a royal escort told Lance his mother could not accompany him. Lance replied, "I don't check my mother at the door." Eventually, the escort relented and took Lance and his mother to meet the king.

Lance competed in the 1996 Tour DuPont for the Motorola Team. At the time, he had no idea that he had cancer.

Everything seemed to be going Lance's way until the 1996 Olympics in Atlanta, Georgia. Lance was favored to win the 138-mile race, but he lost stamina with three laps remaining and finished a disappointing 12th. Lance should have blown away the other riders. Something was wrong, but Lance wouldn't know how wrong until a few weeks later.

Chapter 4
Breaking Through Confusion

Lance was not quite sure what to do with himself once he finished chemotherapy on December 13, 1996. He was not convinced he wanted to return to cycling, and if he didn't, he didn't know what he would do instead. He didn't want to jump into anything until he was sure he was cured of cancer. Doctors continued to monitor his blood and would not consider him out of the woods for another year. While Lance waited in limbo, he decided to start a nonprofit foundation for cancer research. He wanted to repay the doctors who helped save his life and to stay connected with the people in the cancer community who had touched his soul.

Lance formed the Lance Armstrong Foundation with $200,000 from a charitable bicycle race he and some friends organized in March 1997 in Austin, Texas. Today, the annual Ride for the Roses nets more than $1 million and attracts more than 6,000 participants. Events last all weekend and include everything from competitive, amateur, and family bicycle races to a health and sports exposition, a U.S. Postal Service gala dinner, and a silent auction.

Proceeds from the race support the foundation's aim of helping people manage and survive cancer. The foundation focuses on four primary areas: It forms partnerships with leading health institutions and organizations to develop treatment services and support for survivors. It develops public education and awareness programs to encourage early detection of cancer. It provides people with cancer information and support. And, it awards medical and scientific grants to those working to better understand the disease and ultimately to find a cure. As of 2001 the foundation had awarded more than $1 million in grants.

Besides giving Lance a sense of purpose, the foundation also led him to the love of his

He decided to start the Lance Armstrong Foundation to aid cancer research.

life, Kristin Richard. At first, Lance and Kristin, also known as Kik, butted heads. Kik was an account executive for the advertising and public relations firm in Austin that sponsored the Ride for the Roses. She and Lance disagreed during the first race about whether his foundation was doing enough to please her firm. Both have strong personalities, and neither was willing to back down. Eventually the two met in social situations and smoothed out their differences. Lance began to admire Kik's quick wit and intelligence, while Kik saw through Lance's sickly appearance to the fire burning inside him. Within a few months, the two vacationed in Europe, where Lance was proud to show off his language skills in French, Italian, and Spanish. In less than a year they were engaged. Lance was in love and living just for the joy of living for the first time in his life.

Meanwhile, Lance began feeling pressure to return to cycling. Cofidis, a French cycling team, wanted to renegotiate his contract, first while Lance was in the hospital enduring his most difficult round of chemotherapy treatment and later when he finished chemotherapy. The new offer from Cofidis was less than acceptable, so Lance's agent shopped for another contract. No one wanted to hire him. Just when he was ready to give up, a new team showed interest. The U.S. Postal Service team offered Lance a contract that would make a return to cycling worthwhile.

Despite some lingering doubts about cycling, Lance and Kik packed up and moved to Europe with the U.S. Postal Service team in January 1998, shortly after their engagement. After just two pro races in Europe, Lance was ready to quit. He dropped out of an arduous eight-day race through cold and wet mountains in France. He had had enough. He was tired of torturing himself. He wanted to retire from cycling and enjoy life. He and Kik packed up again and moved back home. By then, everyone was worried about Lance. He was not himself. All he did was play golf, water ski, drink beer and eat Mexican food, or lie around on the couch, channel surfing.

Lance, with wife Kristin, waves during the Lance Armstrong parade in Austin, Texas.

"If I ever have any serious problems again, I know I will go back to Boone and find an answer. I got my life back on those rides."

Lance's loved ones were not about to sit back and watch him lose himself. They came up with a bevy of reasons to delay retirement until finally they rekindled his competitive spirit.

Lance's revival came in April 1998 while training with an old friend, Bob Roll, in Boone, North Carolina. Boone is a little hippie town high in the Appalachian mountains, where Lance twice won the Tour Du Pont. In fact, the road to the tour's highest peak, Beech Mountain, still had Lance's name printed on it. Lance came across the words *Viva Lance* and *Go Armstrong* while training on the peak with Roll. The words lifted him out of his cancer blues and set him resolutely back in his saddle.

"I passed the rest of the trip in a state of near reverence for those beautiful, peaceful, soulful mountains," Lance wrote in his autobiography, *It's Not About the Bike: My Journey Back to Life.* "The rides were demanding and quiet, and I rode with a pure love of the bike, until Boone began to feel like a Holy Land to me, a place I had come to on a pilgrimage. If I ever have any serious problems again, I know I will go back to Boone and find an answer. I got my life back on those rides."

Chapter 5
Back on Top

Lance's cycling performance continued to go up and down after his experience in Boone, but he never gave up again. Eventually he started winning races that turned heads in the cycling world. His biggest accomplishment was finishing fourth in October 1998 in the Vuelta a España. Lance rode 2,348 miles over 23 days, and finished just 2 minutes and 18 seconds behind the winner. The feat convinced Lance, and his U.S. Postal Service team director, Johan Bruyneel, that Lance would be a serious contender in the Tour de France the following year.

While Lance set his sites on the Tour, Kik faced some physically grueling challenges as well. She and Lance married in May 1998. By January 1999, they were ready to start work-

Lance and Kristin were married in May 1998.

ing on a family. Getting pregnant was complicated, because chemotherapy had rendered Lance sterile. However, doctors had helped him bank sperm before treatment. They joined that sperm with Kik's eggs and planted an embryo inside Kik through a tedious process called in vitro fertilization. Kik became pregnant by February 1999.

Shortly thereafter, Lance and Kik moved back to Europe so that Lance could train for the Tour de France. Lance was more determined than ever. He and his teammates spent weeks riding the Alps and the Pyrenees mountains they would encounter in the Tour. While other riders were resting or competing in other races, the U.S. Postal Service team was riding seven hours a day, day after day, in all kinds of weather. Lance also went the extra mile on the Col de la Madone, the most difficult ride near his home in Nice, France. The seven-and-a-half-mile climb is so tough that most cyclists ride it only once or twice a season. Lance rode it once a month. He also broke a record for riding the mountain in 31 minutes and 30 seconds. Lance rode it in 30 minutes and 47 seconds. No doubt about it, Lance was ready for the Tour de France.

But was the Tour ready for him? Apparently not. Journalists and other cyclists alike were surprised when Lance started out the

Tour wearing the coveted yellow jersey. The rider in the lead each day wears the yellow jersey. Lance won the jersey the first day for riding the fastest in the prologue, an eight-kilometer time trial at the beginning of the Tour. In fact, riders face three time trials throughout the Tour, and Lance won all three.

Lance Armstrong of the U.S. Postal Team wears the yellow jersey as he passes an American fan during the Tour de France.

Lance is kissed by his mother Linda and wife Kristin after winning the Tour de France on July 25, 1999.

Only three other cyclists had accomplished the same feat in the history of the Tour. By the time the last time trial was over, Lance had established himself as the winner of the 1999 Tour de France. He was too far ahead for other cyclists to catch him in the final stage.

Lance did it. He became the second American to win the Tour and the first member of a U.S. home team to win the Tour, but most importantly he proved to the world that people can thrive after surviving cancer. Fans back in the United States were thrilled. They welcomed him home with bumper stickers that read *Viva La Lance*.

Since then, Lance has won three more Tours—which makes four in a row.

In October 1999 Lance became a father to Luke David Armstrong. Kik also got pregnant again, and gave birth to twin girls, Grace Elizabeth and Isabelle Rose in November 2001. But of all his accomplishments, Lance

Lance celebrates his victory of the Tour de France with his wife Kristin and son Luke on July 23, 2000.

Lance still sees beating cancer as his most defining role.

still sees beating cancer as his most defining role.

"The truth is, if you asked me to choose between winning the Tour de France and cancer, I would choose cancer. Odd as it sounds, I would rather have the title of cancer survivor than winner of the Tour because of what it has done for me as a human being, a man, a husband, a son, and a father," Lance wrote in his autobiography. "The one thing the illness has convinced me of beyond all doubt—more than any experience I've had as an athlete—is that we are much better than we know. We have unrealized capacities that sometimes only emerge in crisis. So if there is a purpose to the suffering that is cancer, I think it must be this: it's meant to improve us. I am very firm in my belief that cancer is not a form of death. I choose to redefine it: it is a part of life."

Lance Armstrong presents President George W. Bush with a yellow U.S. Postal Service jersey in a ceremony at the East Room of the White House in Washington, D.C. on August 3, 2001. Lance's wife Kristin and son Luke also attended. President Bush held the ceremony to honor cancer victims, and he noted that Lance survived testicular cancer to win the prestigious Tour de France three years in a row.

Chronology

1971 - Lance Armstrong is born September 18 in Dallas, Texas, to Linda Mooneyham.

1989 - Chris Carmichael asks Lance to join junior national cycling team and to compete in the Junior World Championships in Moscow, Russia.

1991 - Lance joins the U.S. national cycling team and the Subaru-Montgomery Team.

1992 - Jim "Och" Ochowicz offers Lance a contract with a professional cycling team sponsored by Motorola after watching Lance finish 14th in the Olympics in Barcelona, Spain.

1993 - Rides in and drops out of his first Tour de France. Earns a $1 million bonus for winning three U.S. races in the Thrift Drug Classic. Wins the World Championships in Oslo, Norway.

1995 - Wins a stage in the Tour de France; his teammate Fabio Casartelli dies in a crash on the Tour.

1996 - Lance finishes a disappointing 12th in the Olympics in Atlanta, Georgia. He is diagnosed with testicular and lung cancer on October 2. Later, he learns the cancer has spread to his brain. He finishes three months of chemotherapy on December 13.

1997 - Lance and friends organize first Ride for the Roses to support Lance Armstrong Foundation. Lance meets future wife, Kristin "Kik" Richard.

1998 - Lance and Kik marry. Lance signs a contract with the U.S. Postal Service Pro Cycling Team. He makes an impressive fourth-place finish in the Vuelta a España.

1999 - Wins first Tour de France in July. In October, becomes a father to Luke David.

2000 - Lance wins the Tour de France a second time.

2001 - Lance wins the Tour de France a third time. Kik gives birth to twin girls, Isabelle Rose and Grace Elizabeth.

2002 - wins the Tour de France for the fourth time

2003 - wins second American-International Athlete Trophy

Index